Roaring REPTILES

CREATURES ALL AROUND US

by D. M. Souza

Carolrhoda Books, Inc./Minneapolis

Library of Congress Cataloging-in-Publication Data

Souza, D. M. (Dorothy M.)
     Roaring reptiles / by D.M. Souza.
          p.   cm. — (Creatures all around us)
     Includes index.
     Summary: Describes the physical characteristics, habitat, and life cycle of the crocodilian order, which includes alligators, crocodiles, caimans, and gavials.
     ISBN 0-87614-710-4
     1. Crocodilia—Juvenile literature. 2. Alligators—Juvenile literature. 3. Crocodiles—Juvenile literature. [1. Crocodilia. 2. Alligators. 3. Crocodiles.] I. Title. II. Series: Souza, D. M. (Dorothy M.). Creatures all around us.
     QL666.C9S68   1992
     597.98—dc20   91-31403
                                                                  CIP
                                                                   AC

Manufactured in the United States of America

1 2 3 4 5 6 7 8 9 10 01 00 99 98 97 96 95 94 93 92

This large male alligator can barely be seen above the surface of the water.

Roaring Reptiles

Swimming against the slow-moving current of the river is a creature that looks like a floating log. In an instant, it whips its powerful tail from side to side and thrashes the water. Then it circles back and moves closer to shore.

On top of its head are two bulging eyes with slits like a cat's. At the tip of its long, rounded snout are two steaming nostrils. The creature opens its huge jaws, and its long pointed teeth shine in the sunlight. From deep within its body comes a deafening roar. Birds in the trees scatter.

Meet the alligator. This reptile belongs to a group of animals called crocodilians. The group also includes caimans, crocodiles, and gavials.

Alligators and other crocodilians roamed the earth millions of years ago, along with their relatives the dinosaurs. They have changed little since then. They are the largest of all living reptiles. Some crocodiles in Africa and Australia measure almost 23 feet long. That's longer than a big pickup truck.

All crocodilians look very much alike except for their snouts. Crocodiles' snouts are narrow and almost pointed. Alligators' and caimans' snouts are wide and round. Gavials' are very long and narrow.

If you can ever safely get close to them, you can also tell an alligator and a crocodile apart by their teeth. Both have two large teeth on either side of their lower jaws. Even when the crocodile's mouth is shut, these teeth stick out of its jaw like a bulldog's. In the alligator, they do not poke out. Only the upper teeth show.

4

Crocodilians, like other reptiles, have rows of scales that cover their bodies. Beneath thick pointed scales on their necks, backs, and tails are bony plates called osteoderms (AH-stee-oh-dermz). These plates make their skins, or **hides**, very strong and tough.

Crocodilians do not shed their skins the way other reptiles do. Each scale develops on its own. As the animal grows, new scales grow beneath the old ones and replace them. The scales and bony plates become larger as the reptile grows.

Crocodilians have thick skin covered with scales.

This American alligator, like all crocodilians, is an able swimmer.

All crocodilians are **amphibious** (am-FIH-bee-uhs), that is, they can live both on land and in water. Although they may sun themselves on land for hours, they are most at home swimming, hunting, or hiding in water. There they breathe by keeping their nostrils just above the surface. As they drift along, it's not easy to spot them. They do not even make the water ripple.

7

An alligator warms itself in the sun.

Like all reptiles, crocodilians are cold-blooded, or **ectothermic** (ek-tuh-THUR-mik). This does not mean that their blood is cold, but that their body temperatures change. They do not stay the same, as ours usually do, but go up and down with the temperature of the air and water around them. If it becomes too cold and crocodilians cannot find a sheltered place to hide, many die. This is why most crocodilians live in the tropics or other warm parts of the world.

Many live in Asia, Africa, Australia, and Central and South America. Fish-eating gavials, for example, live in India. Caimans are from Central and South America, but some have been brought into the United States as pets. The young have been sold as baby alligators. When they grow up, they can be vicious.

Most spectacled caimans live in Central and South America, but some have been brought to the United States.

There are fewer than 500 American crocodiles living in Florida's waters.

Two kinds of crocodilians are natives of the United States. The American alligator swims in swampy waters in Florida and several other southeastern states. The American crocodile hides in saltwater marshes around the tip of Florida. It may also swim off the coast of that state.

When crocodilians move swiftly through the water, wildly fight one another, or threaten enemies with tooth-filled jaws, they can be frightening. As we shall see, they are definitely creatures to be admired from a distance.

You probably wouldn't want to meet an alligator as large as this one.

Noisemakers

A 10-foot male alligator stretches out on the bank beside a sluggish stream. As his body warms under the morning sun, water insects buzz around him. Lazily he opens and closes his eyes, but he pays little attention to the insects.

Something else alerts him. It's a noise that sounds like the roar of a huge truck racing its engine. The gator moves his 250-pound body toward the water and slips in. He raises his head and shoulders and draws in large amounts of air through his nostrils.

Another roar, just like the first, comes from the distance. Several blasts bounce back and forth and gradually come closer together. The sound is deafening.

Two male alligators, or **bulls**, face each other in the middle of the stream. Massive jaws open and close as a battle begins. The reptiles twist, turn, and circle each other in the water. They blow air through their nostrils and hiss.

The bull who has been sunning himself on the bank strikes the first blow. He catches the intruder on the shoulder and, with a lightning-quick movement of his powerful tail, flips himself and his victim over. The two thrash about in the water and send fish, frogs, and other small creatures racing for safety.

When his lungs seem almost ready to burst, the gator lifts his tail in the air and lets out a booming roar. The water around him vibrates.

As the gator roars, two glands on each side of his lower jaw open. A musky-smelling chemical called a **pheremone** (FER-uh-mohn) fills the air and floats on the water. The odor will last for several hours and will signal to other gators that this territory already belongs to one male.

These two alligators are about to fight over their territory.

Male crocodilians, such as this American alligator, bellow when they are courting a female.

Finally the intruder cries out "umph, umph." He swims away with a gaping wound above his front leg. The other gator floats on the water and rests after the fight.

Male alligators and other male crocodilians defend their territories during most of the year. They try to keep others, both male and female, out. During mating season, however, females are allowed to enter.

Females sometimes bellow to let bulls know where they are. They may also release musky-smelling pheremones from two glands near their tails. As soon as a male catches this scent from a female, he follows it.

Two alligators prepare to mate.

When the two reptiles meet, the female lets out a loud snort or swims under the bull and blows bubbles. The male may roar back, arch his neck, and wave his tail. He may also give off a pheremone. The two creatures sometimes swim in wild circles or chase one another.

After they mate, the female crocodilian usually leaves the area. She prepares to build a nest and lay her eggs. Soon she will be tending to many young noisemakers in the stream or marsh.

The Nest

Alligators make their nests from uprooted plants.

A female alligator begins building her nest by choosing a place along the bank where shrubs, and grasses grow. She uproots some plants and cuts down others with her teeth. Using her hind feet and tail, she scrapes everything into a heap. If she gets tired, she returns to the water for a while.

After several days, the pile may be 3 feet tall, or as high as a picnic table. Its base may be 6 feet wide—about the size of a wading pool. Female alligators build the biggest nests of all crocodilians.

This alligator nest is almost hidden by tall grasses.

After several days, the pile may be 3 feet tall, or as high as a picnic table. Its base may be 6 feet wide—about the size of a wading pool. Female alligators build the biggest nests of all crocodilians.

Many alligators use the same nests or mounds year after year. They simply add more plants to the top. Old nests are usually larger than new ones.

When the female has collected enough material, she crawls over the nest. She packs it down with mud that she carries in her mouth. Then she digs a small hole near the top, lines it with mud, and begins laying her eggs. As she does, she cups each one with a hind foot so that it rolls gently into the mound hole.

17

She lays about an egg a minute until she has laid between 30 and 60 eggs. Large crocodilians lay more eggs than smaller ones do. The eggs are white, shiny, and about 3 inches long. The shells are thicker than those of a hen's eggs. Beneath each shell is a tough lining called a **membrane** that also covers the tiny developing creature, the **embryo** (EM-bree-oh). Even if the shell breaks, the rubbery membrane protects it.

When the gator finishes laying her eggs, she collects more leaves, mud, and grasses in her mouth and places them on top of the nest. Again she crawls over the mound and uses the weight of her body to press everything down.

Female crocodiles do not build the same kind of nests that alligators do. Some make small mounds of leaves in the shade near the edge of a stream. The American crocodile digs a pit in the sand about 2 feet deep. At night she lays from 40 to 90 eggs in several pits and covers them with more sand.

19

Most crocodilians do not abandon their eggs after laying them as many reptiles do. If raccoons, opossums, or other animals try to rob their nests, the females appear from no-where, hissing and bellowing. The attacker quickly retreats.

As leaves and grasses on the mound rot, they produce heat around the eggs. Sun shining on the sand also warms the eggs. The heat helps the young crocodilians develop, and in two to four months they are ready to hatch.

A female alligator waits in a water hole alongside her nest to protect her eggs.

An American alligator breaks out of its egg.

Help!

A female crocodilian holds her head up out of the water. She listens to the sounds of muffled grunts coming from her nest. As quickly as she can, she moves toward the nest and begins scooping leaves, plants, or sand off the top with her mouth.

A pointed tooth on the tip of the snout helps each young, or **hatchling**, cut through its shell. This tooth falls off within a week.

A newly-hatched American alligator takes its first steps.

Baby gators are about 8 inches long. They are mostly black, with yellow or white rings circling their bodies. Each weighs less than 2 ounces, or about as much as a small candy bar.

Baby crocodiles are greenish gray with black lines crossing their bodies. They are smaller and thinner than baby alligators, but their big heads make them weigh almost as much.

As soon as they are out of the nest, the hatchlings head for the water. Some mothers may even pick up a few babies in their mouths and carry them. The hatchlings are in no danger there. They simply peek out at everything from behind their mother's huge teeth.

Once in the water, the young begin swimming around and swinging their tails from side to side. Some sun themselves on their mother's back. If they have a hard time diving underwater, they swallow small stones or pebbles. These add weight to their bodies.

A baby alligator takes to the water.

At first, the hatchlings eat mostly insects, snails, and small fish. If they spot young mosquitoes, they bend their tails around the insects. Then they scoop them into their jaws.

Female alligators take care of their young for several months. If a female catches a large fish, she crushes it and holds it in her jaws. Then, one by one, the hatchlings break off a piece of the fish with their sharp teeth. They raise their heads, shake the piece of fish several times, and swallow it in one gulp.

If a bird, a raccoon, or another **predator** (PREH-duh-tur)—an animal that hunts them—comes near, young gators may grunt loudly or scream, "umph, umph, umph." Their mother rushes to protect them.

25

A young crocodile gets ready to enter the water.

All young crocodilians grow quickly, about a foot a year during their first two years of life. After that they grow a little more slowly. By the time they are adults, males are a few feet larger and more than 100 pounds heavier than females. But male or female, most are about 7 to 12 feet of reptile dynamite.

Mealtime

This alligator is stalking an unsuspecting bird.

A green-headed duck lands in the middle of a pond. It does not notice the large alligator that is sunning itself along the bank. As the alligator slips silently into the water, the duck turns a somersault, ruffles its feathers, and flutters its wings.

The gator swims noiselessly toward the center of the pond. It nears the bird and sinks lower in the water until only its nostrils show. Then, with a mighty side sweep of its jaws, it grabs the duck and swallows it whole.

Like other crocodilians, the gator does not attack from the front. Instead it swings its open jaws sideways and then snaps down on its victim, or **prey**.

Most crocodilians' front teeth are pointed and are used for snatching and holding onto prey. Teeth in the back are usually dull. They help crush bones and shells. Until the crocodilian grows old, its teeth regularly fall out, and new ones replace them.

This American crocodile, like all crocodilians, has strong teeth and powerful jaws.

Birds are just one type of animal that crocodilians like to eat.

Alligators and other crocodilians are meat eaters, or **carnivores** (KAR-nuh-vorz). They eat animals such as birds, mammals, and fish. Sometimes large crocodilians even eat smaller ones. They are said to be **cannibals** because they eat their own kind.

Most of the time crocodilians catch their victims in the water. For example, if a muskrat, wild hog, or other animal comes to the edge of the water for a drink, an alligator will race toward it. It will grip its prey in its jaws, drag it underwater, and hold it there until it drowns. If the animal is too large to swallow whole, the gator will tear it apart and gulp it down piece by piece. Its digestive juices are powerful enough to dissolve bones, hair, and tough or scaly skin.

This alligator will carry its half-eaten prey in its jaws until it is hungry enough to finish eating.

Several things make it possible for crocodilians to stay under water without drowning. Behind their mouths are special folds of skin. Underwater, these folds close, sealing off water from their lungs. They also have flaps of skin behind their nostrils that close and keep water from entering their throats.

Even though these creatures look as if they would have huge appetites, they do not. They move slowly and spend much of their time resting. They rarely have to hunt very long or go very far because fish, turtles, snakes, birds, frogs, or other animals are usually close by. So they do not need much energy from a large amount of food.

It is not unusual for some crocodilians to hold prey in their jaws for several hours. If they are not hungry, they will carry the food around until they are ready to eat.

An alligator rests in its water hole.

Water Holes

One morning a young alligator begins building a den. It moves slowly to a spot along the bank of a stream. With its snout and its webbed feet, it scoops out dirt and mud. It pushes these to the side with its hind feet and tail. Plants and grasses are either uprooted or packed down. Now and then, the reptile swishes its tail and pushes loose items downstream. In time, the den will fill with water.

Alligators use water holes to protect their young from predators.

Crocodilians build dens or water holes to hide from danger or watch for passing meals. They frequently use the same dens year after year. Many females build their nests near dens so that they can guard the nests from their hiding places. When their eggs hatch, they bring their young to these hideouts to protect them from predators.

As they stay motionless in their dens, the reptiles don't need to breathe as often as we do. But when they do, they don't always swim to the surface. Instead they use several openings they have dug in the muddy roofs of their water-filled dens. By poking their snouts through these holes, they catch a breath of air.

Most crocodilians live in climates that are warm year round. Some American alligators, however, live in areas where the temperatures can become cool. They use their dens for winter shelters. The holes can be 40 feet deep and up to 10 feet wide at the entrance.

During cold spells the alligator's body systems slow down. It breathes very little, and its heart beats only a few times each minute. It has extra fat stored in its body from summer feedings, so it does not have to hunt.

Once in a while on a sunny day, a gator may leave its winter home to warm itself on shore. But as soon as the weather becomes chilly, it goes back inside where the temperature is warmer than the air outside.

An alligator suns itself beside its water hole.

This water hole has begun to dry out, and the alligator who uses it will soon have to dig for more water.

Water holes are a help not only to crocodilians but also to many other creatures living nearby. When a crocodilian builds or enlarges its den, many insects, small shellfish, and water plants are stirred up and rise to the surface. There they become food for other hungry animals.

During dry months, when water in streams and marshes is low, crocodilians dig deeper into the mud and sometimes find more water underground. Birds, turtles, frogs, and mammals come to the water holes for a drink. Fish crowd together as tightly as sardines in a can. Of course, a few of these creatures end up in the crocodilian's stomach. But none of them would survive if it were not for the reptile's water hole.

34

Hide hunters value the skins of crocodilians, but hunting has greatly reduced the number of crocodilians in the world.

In Danger

Over one hundred years ago, large numbers of alligators and crocodiles lived in and around our southeastern states. Many alligators could even be found swimming up the Mississippi River. But then hunters began killing them.

People called hide hunters discovered that the skins of the reptiles could be made into expensive boots, shoes, belts, and handbags. Other hunters took the eggs from nests and sold them to people who liked to eat them. Soon there were fewer baby crocodilians hatching, and many of those that did hatch were killed and turned into stuffed toys.

When crocodilians began disappearing in alarming numbers, laws were passed that made it a crime to kill them. The crocodilian population slowly came back, and limited hunting is allowed.

But the reptiles now face another threat. Their **habitats** (HA-buh-tats), the marshes and streams where they live, are being drained to make room for new buildings, towns, and cities. Crocodilians now have fewer places to swim, hide their eggs, or build their dens.

There are almost no Siamese crocodiles left in nature. Most, including the one pictured here, live in zoos.

In the United States, many crocodilians, including this alligator, live in areas where their lives and habitats are protected.

Unless we do everything we can to protect them and their surroundings, these mighty creatures may someday be lost. They may follow the path of their relatives, the great dinosaurs, who disappeared from the earth millions of years ago.

Scientists who study animals group them together according to their similarities and differences. These groups are given names in Latin. Animals that have certain features in common are placed in the same order. Crocodilians belong to an order of reptiles known as Crocodilia. Within the order, there are three different families. Below are some of the members of these families and a few facts about them.

FAMILY	EXAMPLES	LARGEST	WHERE FOUND
Alligatoridae	American alligator Chinese alligator spectacled caiman	19 feet, 2 inches 4 feet 9 feet	United States China Central and South America and Florida
Crocodylidae	American crocodile saltwater crocodile	23 feet 24 feet, 4 inches	United States and South America India
Gavialidae	gavial (or gharial)	21½ feet	India

Glossary

amphibious: able to live both on land and in water

bulls: male crocodilians

cannibals: animals that eat their own kind

carnivores: animals that eat the meat of other animals

ectothermic: having a body temperature that changes depending on the temperature of the environment

embryo: the young of an animal in the beginning stages of its development

habitats: places where a type of animal lives

hatchling: a newborn animal such as a crocodilian

hides: animals' skins

membrane: a thin layer of skin or tissue

pheremone: a substance that certain animals, including crocodilians, give off to send a signal to other animals of the same species

predator: an animal that hunts and eats other animals

prey: an animal that is killed and eaten by other animals

Index

The photographs are reproduced through the courtesy of: pp. 3, 9, 10, 25, 26, 27, 28 30, 37, front cover, back cover, © J. H. Robinson; pp. 5, 6, Wendy W. Cortesi; pp. 1 (left), 7, 11, 12, 14, 16, 31, 32, 33, 35, © Connie Toops; pp. 8, 17, 23, © Cheryl Koenig Morgan; p. 15, © Gerard Lemmo; pp. 18, 20, 21, 22, 29, 34, © Tom Cawley; pp. 1 (right), 36, Thomas C. Boyden.